RECESSION MILLIONAIRE

Build Wealth, Not Fear

E.A. Davidson

All rights to this book are reserved. No permission is given for any part of this book to be reproduced, transmitted in any form or means; electronic or mechanical, stored in a retrieval system, photocopied, recorded, scanned, or otherwise. Any of these actions require the proper written permission of the publisher.

Copyright © 2019, E.A. Davidson

Disclaimer

All erudition contained in this book is given for informational and educational purposes only. The author is not in any way accountable for any results or outcomes that emanate from using this material. Constructive attempts have been made to provide information that is both accurate and effective, but the author is not bound for the accuracy or use/misuse of this information.

Contents

INTRODUCTION 6

CHAPTER ONE 13

  RECESSION 13

    Recession Indicators 19

    Types of Recession 22

CHAPTER TWO 27

  THE MINDSET OF A MILLIONAIRE 27

    Tips to Developing the Right Mindset 30

CHAPTER THREE 39

  MAKING MONEY FROM FINANCIAL CRISES .. 39

    What To Do 41

    The Bottom Line 51

CHAPTER FOUR 53

  TOP BILLIONAIRES WHO HAVE MADE MONEY DURING RECESSION 53

    Warren Buffett 56

Sergey Brin 58

John Paulson 59

Jamie Dimon 60

Steven Schonfeld 61

Andrew Beal 62

Carl Icahn 63

CONCLUSION 67

MAINTAINING YOUR SUCCESS 67

INTRODUCTION

2008 was the first time I ever came across the word "Recession." I did not fully understand what it meant, but it sent cold chills down my spine to realize that a lot of business owners were scared of making losses. A lot of other people were scared of the increase in unemployment that may come with the period. However, the recession did not come with so much good. It came with more bad than good. Many businesses hibernated indefinitely; companies retrenched a lot of their staff members. Some others had their job offers canceled. Everywhere reeked of fear. After some time, things went back to normal. People were smiling again, and the recession was over. For a moment, it had felt like life was coming to an end.

From that experience, I got to understand how terrible things can get during the period. But then, there were a few questions that popped in my head a few times. Why does recession have to happen? What happens if it takes longer than usual before it ends? Are there possible long-lasting damages that occur to the system even after the period is over? The most important question amongst all was how to survive and make money during a recession. I bet you are eager for answers to these questions.

Over the years, the world economy has faced several financial crises. There is usually a global economic downturn in almost every eight years, and it comes like an apocalypse when people lose jobs and businesses fall. Did you know that, during this period, it is possible to benefit hugely from the situation? Did you also know that despite the financial slump, people still make millions? The answers to these questions are affirmative and this is the crux of the matter in this book. The possibility of making money and comfortably surviving a pecuniary collapse may sound unreal, but it is true. In this book, you will learn about how you can maximize the opportunities available such that your endeavors produce success.

Remarkably, this last decade has endured so many economic disasters in different parts of the world and it has also witnessed the rise of millionaires to billionaires. How is that even possible? I also had the same question as you.

The stock exchange market grossly contributed to the rise of millionaires around the world. The number of millionaires increased by 17% to 10 million, with their combined fortune surged by 19% to $39 trillion. This upturn signifies that a considerable amount has been recovered from the losses of the last economic breakdown. The value of stocks and bonds levitated a great deal and investment firms were able to recuperate their losses.

The swiftest development in fortune notably occurred in China, Brazil, India and a lot of other nations that took hard hits from the 2008 recession. Particularly, Asia had an enormous trade and industry enlargement that matched Europe's economy for the first time and a lot of nations in the Latin American region recorded all-time highs in their wealth structures.

The cumulative riches of Asia's top millionaires heaved by 31 percent to $9.7 trillion as they outshined Europe millionaires whose accumulated fortune rested at $9.5 trillion. In North America, the rich statuses multiplied by an astounding 17% and their collective wealth was worth about $10.7 trillion at an 18% increase.

The United States of America maintained its position as the household of the highest amount of world millionaires with almost 3 million people. Japan followed with 1.65 million people, Germany had 861,000 and China had about 477,000 people in the millionaire circle. Switzerland also had an extraordinary population of rich and wealthy people with a ratio of 35 in 1,000 grownups.

Mind you, all these statistics stated above were recorded within the last decade. Are you still wondering if it is possible to be part of these millionaires and billionaires that push the global economic wagon forward?

During the period when situations began to turn around, financiers maintained caution in their transactions due to the wrecks caused by the collapse that expunged stock gains which had been amassed for years, wheeled unemployment to a raise and contributed to the shrinkage of the global economy.

With the expense of cautious dealings, moguls still spent a lot of their money on substantial fixed-income investments such as real estate and other freights in an ongoing quest for predictable earnings and liquidity of cash.

The recession made a lot of business magnates smarter in their wealth and investment management. I believe this gives hope that rather than panic during a disastrous period, weigh your options and find a way out of it. Evaluate your ideas properly before venturing into it.

Millionaire families that used to save their monies in closer securities began to set feet on the developing economies of foreign nations and that is why many financiers across Europe and North America are found to be exposing themselves to Asian markets which are foreseen to be prospects of the world's largest economy.

For better understanding, I am going to compare the importance of money to blood in the human body. The heart is responsible for the pumping and circulation of blood, which makes it a vital necessity for life. You and I know what will happen if the heart stops working. It means death even when there is blood in the body. This is what happens during a recession. It is a state of economic collapse. Invariably, it means that once the heart of a country stops circulation money, many parts of the economy will suffer gradually till the nation plunges to death.

In the human chain of coexistence, there is a need for relationships that involve the exchange of valuable commodities. There is always a need to satisfy and there are people on the other end who can provide these needs at certain expenses. These providers also have workers who help with the processes of making the needs available and are being paid for their services. The workers also have needs that will be met with the money being paid for their services. This is how the cycle of business continues to flow. If the demand for these needs decreases, the providers will also decrease their productions and workers. Thus, the decline in the market. Therefore, a recession happens where there is a downturn in business activities.

CHAPTER ONE

RECESSION

If you have been lucky enough to witness a storm or a whirlwind, you would understand how powerless everything becomes when it occurs. The heavy rains flood everywhere while the breeze comfortably displaces anything it can lay its hands upon. Recession can be likened to a perfect storm that upsets economic activities such that you can hardly control the situation. You can only complain about it. It will still wreck its intended havoc. When the financial storm occurs, it affects all and sundry, leaving no parts of the business sphere untouched.

When a recession happens, it means there is a general deterioration in the economic doings of a business cycle. It usually spans a couple of months with visible adverse developments in GDP, income, industrial trade and even employment.

Commonly, the economic downturn occurs when the demand faces a hostile blow. The decrease in order will lead to a reduction in supply, thereby truncating the liquid flow of cash in the economy. This fatal blow is usually dealt by different situations such as financial crises, catastrophic international trade, socioeconomic quandaries, or an adversative supply tremor that is capable of diminishing demand. Several governments around the world have adopted possible solutions to this stormy situation. These solutions include reduction of tax rates, an upturn in money distribution amongst other inflated macroeconomic strategies.

People often talk about vehicles and how they can develop faults at any point, but what they always ignore is the signs that had been showing on the dashboard before the fault aggravated enough to break it down. For every vehicle that breaks down midway a journey, it must have given signs to the driver who must have perceived as regular. This also happens with recession. A lot of times, a recession is caused by the bleaks in the economy. These signs contribute primarily to the massive decline in industrial activities.

The least duration of an economic catastrophe spans for nothing less than six months and it usually affects five significant parts of the economy: the GDP, manufacturing industry, merchandising sales, revenue and employment.

I know that you probably have read or been taught that recession only occurs when there is a successive negative growth rate in the GDP that lasted two or more quarters. That is true. But another truth is that the downturn can start unnoticed before the trimestral gross internal product reports are available. These factors should be monitored just as you have to monitor the red signals of your vehicle because the degeneration of economic indicators triggers the degeneration of the GDP.

Recession never comes in as a shock. It habitually commences after numerous quarters of deceleration that are masked with optimistic progression. Regularly, there will be trimestral periods of negative growth in the economy with positive seasonal developments in between, but we tend to focus on these positives.

The manufacturing sector is always the first economic indicator of an imminent recession. Manufacturers are providers of needs and they produce based on the intensity of the demand. To meet up with the market, they have to employ adequate hands to match orders. Therefore, once there is a deterioration in the global demand, production automatically deepens, and unemployment gradually sets in. This will drag the economy.

The deterioration in consumer order is usually the primary cause of negative growth. The descent in sales deters economic expansion and speeds up the unemployment rate. This way, recession slowly creeps in.

The effects of recession are not only limited to business owners or financial workers alone. You may think that you are immune to the consequences because you do not sell stuff or because you are a freelancer who is not on a payroll budget and so, are not worried about being laid off due to the decline in employment. Here is what you need to know. You, as a freelancer, are a part of the economy and recession does not leave out any part. It affects all. As an outworker, you have clients who you provide with your services and they are also in the business cycle. They can only conveniently reward you of your services when they have earned from the system.

Sometimes, the consequences of recession are usually long-lasting than expected. Let me share an instance with you. I know a man who lived through the 2008 recession as an inventory analyst for a firm. He was not the only one in that position as they had three other people doing the same duties. When the recession kicked off, the other three people were relieved of their duties because the firm had to reduce staff capacity. So, this man was left to do the work of four people. After the recession ended and things returned to normal, they did not employ people to fill the voids. They did not see the need to. Other departments got new additions while some people got their jobs back but at lower pay rates. This is how terrible recession can be. Hence, the reason you have to prepare for the period.

Meanwhile, there is the need to use the proficiency of economy administrators to define the state of the country to avoid getting encumbered by numbers. These administrators will verify through monthly data if the country is in recession or not. This enables precision and appropriate dimensions.

Recession Indicators

1. **Gross Domestic Products** – Some countries may consider this as the most significant recession indicator. This is because it calculates the combined economic output of all the individuals and businesses that exist within a specific economy. The GDP can signal a recession when it exhibits an adverse growth proportion. In some cases, the initial negative growth may turn out positive in the following three months of business. Other situations may need the nation's body of analysts to evaluate the reports of the subsequent quarterly GDP estimates. This evaluation covers the data for five months. This allows for a practical assessment of commercial evolution. The absence of progress in these economic signals will immensely affect the GDP; they have to be closely monitored in order to predict the occurrence of a recession.

2. **Real Income** - Real income gauges the personal income of businesses and individuals

attuned for inflation. The income rate of the citizens can determine the level of demand in commodities and when demand is stumpy due to low-income rate, production suffers. The way you crave things will change when your income compared to the value of things have a significant difference ratio.

3. **Employment** - Employment is also considered as a recession indicator because this is what compounds the workforce of the economy. In a situation whereby there are many unemployed people, the scale of preference will address the demand for their needs more than wants. Imagine that you shop for groceries monthly and you love to buy different types of bread-spread for variety purposes. If you lose your job, it means your income is affected and that will affect your spending and so, rather than shop for variety, you begin to shop for preference.

4. **Manufacturing and Wholesale/Retail trade –** This indicator is another essential one as it embodies

the production unit of the economy. This is the part of the economy that is responsible for the provision of consumer needs. Once you stop buying the other bread-spreads, the company producing it will have to reduce their production in order to cut their losses. The size of the workforce required then deepens and so, liquidity of funds begin to slack. This amounts to a recession.

Contrary to popular opinion, the stock market is not a recession indicator. This is because the market is more unstable than a nation's economy due to the imbalance in Investors' expectations. Some investors appear positive and others, negative.

Nonetheless, the stock market can also cause a recession. This happens when a larger population of investors withdraw their investments due to pessimism and lack of confidence in a particular economy.

Types of Recession

However, recession exists in different types and these variations are the determinants of the duration, intensity and consequences of the economic issue.

1. Boom And Bust Recession

This type of recession occurs in the aftermath of an economic boom. A boom happens when there is an unusual positive growth in the economy. It is usually untenable because the boom triggers inflation. For instance, it is your first time of patronizing the newly-opened pizza outlet in your neighborhood and on taking the first bite, you realize how delicious it is, compared to the regular ones you order from the farther outlet you used to buy. It becomes more impressive when you realize that it is cheaper.

During a hangout with friends, you recommend the pizza and they love it too. This means that the customer base of the outlet increases by the day and then, it multiplies such that people start to form queues to grab a bite. When there is an increase in the customer base, the cost of products will increase. This upsurge in price and demand may affect the quality of the pizza because the outlet now begins to focus more on profit rather than satisfying the significant need for quality food. When this happens, the demand gradually drops and so does the production. This drop is as a result of the unsustainable boom experienced by the outlet.

In situations whereby the economic affluence forces the inflation out of control, the central bank takes advantage by imposing higher interest rates and higher taxes in order to increase revenue and decrease expenditure.

At this stage, the saving ratio of the consumer reduces and the debt rate increases. This then, causes the attitude of a consumer to change from spending to debt payment. Automatically, the demand falls.

However, this type of recession can be ephemeral as the increased interest rates can be decreased for the recovery of the economy. It can also be avoided by ensuring that the inflation rate is low.

2. Balance Sheet Recession

Banks and financial companies often cause a balance sheet recession. This occurs when there is a drop in the value of assets, which causes loss of money. It also happens when there are bad loans. These situations mean that these firms are running at huge losses which habitually cause unevenness in their balance sheets and so, investments will be limited in the bid to equate a balance. The drop in investments leads to recession. It is otherwise known as the credit crunch. For instance, if there is a fall in the value of houses and landed properties, it will affect consumer net-worth, which increases bank deficits.

This type of recession often lasts long as the reversal of interest rates may not effect a recovery, thereby leading to a liquidity trap. However, it can be eluded by ensuring that asset values do not simmer.

3. Depression

Also known as a double-dip recession, a depression is an elongated downturn in economic activities where the GDP drastically falls and employment rate soars exceptionally high. This type of recession can be caused by the extended impact of the balance sheet recession. Once an economy suffers a lack of investments for too long, it falls into depression.

4. Supply-Side Shock Recession

This type of recession occurs when the GDP is low due to the truncated output caused by the deterioration in consumer standard of living. For instance, when an economy depends majorly on a product, inflation may cause the lower output often known as 'stagflation.' But this is quite uncommon as there is hardly any economy that is dependent on a particular product to boost GDP.

5. Demand-Side Shock Recession

This is also an unusual situation where the output is low despite the absence of inflation. This may occur due to consumers' lack of assurance in the economy.

Furthermore, different shapes are used to describe the types of recession. They are:

- **W Shaped Recession** – This occurs when a recession ensues right after the recovery of a previous one.

- **V Shaped Recession** – This describes the imminent recovery from an economic fall.

- **L Shaped Recession** – This describes the situation whereby the positive growth is slow, and the rate of unemployment is still high even after recovery.

Conclusively, there is only one beneficial fact about recession, and this revolves around its ability to prevent inflation.

CHAPTER TWO

THE MINDSET OF A MILLIONAIRE

Today's millionaires are not born with a secret code infused in their DNA on how to be successful. There is nothing they know that others cannot uncover. The only segregating line here is the culture of imbibing the right habits and attitude. Thoughts they say, create words, words create actions, and actions create patterns which then orchestrate realities. As Robert Kiyosaki rightly said, *"your future is created by what you do today and not what you do tomorrow."* In as much as your actions are dependent on your thoughts, it is imperative you start thinking like a millionaire if you want to become one. Being a millionaire more often than not is a product of prosperous seeds sown in your thought life with the aim of transcribing your actions into principles that produce profound financial success stories. The more significant part of being wealthy does not come from what you do daily. Instead, it comes from your in-depth knowledge about money making, as well as the mentality you have as regards your time and goals.

Robert Kiyosaki fondly explained the importance of this subject matter in his famous quote saying, _"Financial freedom is available to those who learn about it and work for it."_ Are you enthusiastic about financial freedom? If so, it is time you start seeking financial education because the desire and the motive are as ultimately vital to the achievement of financial success.

The millionaires' minds focus on certain paradigms, which are essential to developing the right mindset, as well as overcoming limiting thoughts and beliefs. You have to seek knowledge of skill development and effective money management and creative spontaneity. Robert Kiyosaki also said, _"The reason_ *positive thinking alone does not work is that most people went to school and never learned how money works, so they spend their lives working for money."* This explains that the actions themes of developing a successful mindset and working towards actualizing your dreams, inherently work hand in hand, as only thinking and dreaming about a being a millionaire definitely will lead to stagnancy. You have to ensure your thoughts impact your actions positively so as to nudge you in the right direction.

It all starts with a dream. You must desire to be financially successful. This desire is the driving force that sets the process in motion. There are certain millionaire mindsets tips which can help you translate your actions into values to adopt in order to set yourself up for success.

Tips to Developing the Right Mindset

1. Dream Big

Being a successful person involves way more than you may think or expect. There is a question that interviewers often ask their candidates during an interview session which is "How do you view yourself in the next five years?" or "What are your dreams and ambitions?" These questions carry more weight than you may understand. This is because they hope to know how big your dreams are. One important factor about your goals is that it is the primary drive force of your zeal to succeed. You can start small, but you have to think big. You have to be able to audaciously visualize what you want to achieve on a large scale without being obstructed by inherent limits. Positivity is the word here; you must make sure to think, feel, and act positively even in the face of adverse circumstances. On the road to becoming a millionaire, you would often encounter obstacles which can raise reasons for you to doubt your dream, skills, and confidence. You can overcome this by fragmenting your vision into an executable action plan, with the full cognizance of the capacity of your challenges. This will help you provide a smart solution plan.

"Opportunity is missed by most people because it is dressed in overalls and looks like work." - Thomas Edison

2. Define Your Goal and Have A Vision.

Achieving great financial feat is almost impossible without setting firm goals. For a student to successfully ace an examination, he has to study extensively. For success to be assured, you have to set attainable goals. Setting lofty goals will give you the right push to chase your dreams head on. You should never be afraid to go after your desires, and your fears can raise doubts that may deter your success. Therefore, you must ensure that you create actions coupled with the right attitude channeled towards achieving set goals. Your goals must be SMART. A 'SMART' goal is a "**S**pecific, **M**easurable, **A**ttainable,

Relevant and Time-framed goal." This means that your intentions have to be well-defined, determinate, realistic and time framed. Specific goals are well defined such that they are void of all forms of vagueness. Do not harbor an equivocal idea of what you want to achieve. Make them specific. For instance, setting a goal to save up $500 per month within a year in order to raise funds to set up your first workshop is more specific and measurable than merely stating 'I want to start a business at the end of the year.' By this, you know the overall you hope to have at the end of the year, and so, you can efficiently work towards it. Stating your goals without a vision makes them ambiguous, which usually ends up being just a dream. A well-defined goal attracts your financial success story, and it sure must be time bound to ensure periodical reviews for necessary adjustments.

3. Hone Your Skills and Never Stop Learning

A popular quote made by Amit Kalantri goes, *"Schooling doesn't assure employment, but skill does."* A critical feature of a positive life is the need for continuous improvement. I firmly believe that every human is born with an innate skill set and the ability of assimilation. This ability helps to redefine and improve the natural talents that you already possess. Chris Matakas emphasizes that *"Mastery lies on an infinite continuum, and as a result, we will never reach the end. We can, however, see to it that we are as far along that continuum as our circumstance allows."* This further explains the essential need for you to continue learning new things for as long as you can. There is no human existing with infinite knowledge. There is a need to concentrate on your field of excellence. Are you yet to discover your area of strength? If your answer is affirmative, then you can find yourself by paying attention to the things you are good at. You can also discover this by asking questions and seeking feedback from your friends, colleagues, and family members. Millionaires always have value to offer, so you must ensure you always ooze of substance. Do not embrace mediocrity. Use the lessons acquired from mentors and coaches to develop your existing skills. In other words, _"never rest on your oars, never stop learning."_ Perhaps it is time for you to seek a more profound financial education. Money is one form of power but having the right knowledge and mentality will enrich you with more energy. Money comes and goes, but with the right mind and skill set, you can successfully build wealth without the fear of failure.

4. Be Passionate

Of the numerous actions to take towards developing a millionaire mindset, being passionate is a vital point. Robert G. Allen said, _"Pursuing your passion is fulfilling and leads to financial freedom."_ In the course of your journey to wealth and success, you will be faced with different challenges, but you must develop a skin-deep attitude and be passionately focused. Imagine that you start a business according to your plan which you have meticulously evaluated, and your expectations do not quite match your present circumstance, this is the time to develop the discipline of delayed gratification and not the time to give in. Your passion for a successful result will egg you on. DEVELOP PASSION AND RESILIENCE!

5. Develop Excellent Time and Money Management Skills.

This factor is an essential skill that you must develop. Being a millionaire does not entail poor spending habits and abysmal time value. To develop a millionaire mindset, you have to be time conscious because opportunities come with time and so, you cannot let your chances slide by through complacency. How do you currently spend your time and money? Do you often buy things you want rather than the things you need? Do you have a saving habit? Do your idle hours of leisure occupy the better parts of your days? I urge that you provide honest answers to these questions within yourself as they will help you identify where you need to effect changes. Time can be likened to a banknote that you cannot retrieve once you spend it. You have to be careful enough to ensure that whatever you spend your time on is productive and beneficial to your life goals. Time is a precious resource that you must manage wisely to achieve the optimum result. The less time you waste on fruitless activities, the more effective and productive you become. Being productive will make you successful as you will continuously work towards actualizing your ideas. Your ability to actively capitalize on your potentials within an available time will influence how fast you rise to the peak of your success. In other words, time is money; invest it wisely. While consciously working towards your time management, you should also be focusing on adjusting your saving culture and spending habit. These two factors are intertwined as your spending conversely affects your savings. In order to enable an excellent saving habit, you need to manage your spending. Conservation is a beautiful habit to be imbibed in your financial life. Warren Buffet's quote that says, _"Do not save what is left after spending but spend what is left after saving"_ wise saying because that can help you dictate what to do with your money. However, saving is the easiest way of accumulating adequate funds for investments. An investment is an asset which generates more an income over time. Investments can be starting a business, buying stocks, venturing in real estate, or anything which will create a stream of income. It is, however, wise to keep a reasonable fraction of your savings aside for unexpected financial emergencies. You must invest time in your financial education to build with a solid foundation. This emphasizes the need for your mind to be strengthened and shaped right through education, be it formal or informal.

6. Think Long-Term

Being a millionaire is not something that can be achieved in a day or two. This is a feat that can only be accomplished gradually over a period of time.

Making money overnight signifies that you can also lose it within a twinkle of an eye. But if you are able to focus your energy on developing a long-lasting wealth, your chances of failing reduce to the barest minimum. A lot of start-up companies have faltered within a short period of operations because they focused on quick profits rather than long-term growth. You have to understand that success does not come fast and easy. You have to work and build over a long time so that you can project and avoid the errors that could affect you in the future. In the beginning, it may seem fruitless and vile, but you need to continue to push because these are the periods where you need to relax and learn without a rush. Looking to achieve your goals within a short period will make you venture into activities that have weak foundations. By now, the famous saying, *"Rome was not built in a day"* should make more sense to you. Being and staying successful takes time, hard work and resilience.

Conclusively, developing a millionaire mindset starts with you. There are numerous ideas and advice shared on different platforms about what to do to achieve success, but the most critical factor is that you must be prepared for all comes with it. The easiest way to get by is by having the mindset of a millionaire.

CHAPTER THREE

MAKING MONEY FROM FINANCIAL CRISES

If you have the opportunity of searching the memories of many investors, you would realize that the mental pictures of the last recession are still fresh. The ruins that came with the period left scars on many lives and businesses. Retirement plans were shattered, and career developments went into comas. Situations got worse because people overreacted to the financial downturn. Many thought (and probably still think) that the recession was the Armageddon. You probably are one of these people and that is why you are reading this book. Would you believe if I told you that amidst all the panic, some people made millions off the disastrous time? It may be hard for you to believe but, a lot of tolerant and systematic investors took advantage of the period as an opportunity.

I once read about a businessman who lost about 35% of his net worth due to the economic downturn and this will make him either dread the period for the rest of his life or find a hack to it. Of course, you would choose to find a solution rather than live in fear of the inevitable.

Capitalizing on a crisis is unequivocally unsafe especially when you are not certain of the recovery time. Making money during this period might come off as a slightly tricky task but it is a real possibility. You can simply end up smiling real big when the economy recovers just by taking that leap of faith without allowing panic and fear of loss to ruin your chances.

What To Do

1. Grab the Bull By The Horn

During the course of the uproar caused by a recession, prices of assets usually plunge deeper than it should and so, it causes a lot of people to sell their properties in fear of making huge losses due to devaluation. Careful investors usually see this as an opportunity to add to their pile of assets by acquiring the properties at cheaper rates with the hope that when the economy recovers, the assets regain their value. When these happen, it is a win for the investor who buys because, the worth of assets revert to original statuses or might even worth more. In some cases, the sales of real estate assets during this period, are caused by fear and are the reasons for the diminish in worth because these impatient financiers are eager to sell off before the properties further decline in value. However, for you to profit from a financial catastrophe, you need to be calm, disciplined, patient and importantly, you need to possess adequate liquid resources in order to easily procure the unscrupulous acquisitions that are available.

You would have realized by now that fear and anxiety is one of the major causes of the wrecks that come with an economic breakdown. Whenever a downturn occurs, stockholders often cause an unrest in the market through panic. Once there is an unrest, stocks and bonds suffer too. Meanwhile, prices always bounce back to original rates or higher when things get back to normal and by this time, the impatient stockholders who had disposed their assets will look to buy them back at higher rates. If you ask me, I will consider that as a loss. Historically, studies on crises that have happened within past one hundred years, have shown that the overreaction of market participants is the major cause of financial fatalities.

During the World War II, the stock market index recorded a drastic fall from 4% which it had initially fell to, to 18% in a matter of months. However, when the war ended, the market experienced an average rise of 25% per year. This signifies that you can keep a cool head during similar modern occurrences that initiate financial disasters such that you conveniently acquire stocks and assets at giveaway prices.

As at 2019, the stock market continues to enjoy bull market that has spanned over six years already. Investors who acquired assets during the last recession have been able to extend their gains while the impatient and anxious lots are still lamenting over their sorrows. This is a way to take advantage of a financial crisis. Rather than panic, you should look to invest. It is a risk that involves high chances of winning.

Nonetheless, investing in the stock exchange market is certainly not the only way of profiting from a recession. You can also take advantage of the situation by capitalizing in the real estate and housing markets. This market is another big victim of financial crises. During the period of commercial meltdown, houses lose their worth and many mortgages face foreclosure. When this happens, it is a great opportunity to acquire properties of good quality for low prices as they will yield substantial profits when the market is stabilized. The major action you should take is to exercise calmness, caution and then, prepare enough funds for these opportunities.

2. Be Diplomatic. (Accept The Absence Of Profits And Avoid Losses)

In as much as you look to trade for profits during a financial crisis, you should also understand that you may not make profits. In fact, if the crisis lingers than normal, you may have to sell off some risk assets. But one thing you should ensure to maintain is the absence of losses. If you cannot make profits, then you should endeavor to not make losses too.

The recovery time of an economic recession is usually unknown to many, especially if it is a double dip recession. Hence, the need for you to be diplomatic.

You need to make sure that you maintain a low risk exposure in your asset management just in case things do not turn out as envisaged. For instance, you need to know the right property to acquire in order to purchase one that made not yield as much as others would when the economy recovers.

According to behavioral finance, people actually get into their emotions when an economic recession occurs, and this is part of the causes of poor choices. Therefore, when others are rushing into decisions, be diplomatic enough to understand your odds before placing your bets. Taking unprotected risks will further increase the extent of your losses.

3. Know what to invest in.

Your ability to decipher what to invest in will also boost your chances of making money during financial crises. This is because there are certain assets that gain value just as the market drops. These assets vary from treasury bonds to raw materials like gold and oil.

Using the US Treasury bond as an instance, investors usually make efforts to protect the bonds when there is crisis. This is due to its sensitivity to interest rates when it the situation spans for long. Investing in treasury bonds will give you an upside such that you continue to enjoy a smooth and favourable rate even when things get back to normal. Treasury bonds are one of the few soft assets that do not suffer devaluation during crises.

Raw materials such as, gold and oil amongst others, are hard assets that usually enjoy increases in value during downturns. Although, these assets do not produce specific earnings or dividends, they can be traded at valuable rates. This is because hard assets often become scarce during downturns. Hard assets become more treasured when economic crises plunge deeper.

If you are able to understand the strategic steps to take towards investing during a commercial crunch, you may never need to fear or panic when it happens.

In the meantime, you also need to understand the dynamics of the market before making such investments.

Investing in real estate is also one of the best options when considering what to invest in. There is often low risk and high profit in this business. During a recession, prices of buildings ridiculously fall and purchasing them at their vulnerable prices will increase your net-worth when they regain their value.

4. Build Yourself

This topic is generally useful to all categories of readers, but it is more beneficial to employees. As an individual, one thing that makes you stand out from the regular people is your skill. You have to be marketable and valuable in whatever position you find yourself. So far, we have gone back and forth about people who have lost their jobs due to the disastrous economic situation. But do you know that there are people who retain their jobs even when companies and firms are actively retrenching? These people maintain their positions because they have built themselves to be extremely treasurable and indispensable such that they are not affected by the rumblings that may be going on.

One important thing to note is that you are your biggest income and so, you must make extra efforts at selling yourself by improving on your skills and abilities and also acquiring additional expertise that will be useful to you. It is good to also strive to excellently develop good relationships between clients and colleagues, and also maintain internal benevolence.

Adding to your skill set may involve getting more degrees or professional certifications. These are the factors that make you bankable. Building yourself should also involve the enhancement of your creativity. People often like people who can make things happen. This is one of the important ways to amass success during a financial crisis because being resourceful will earn you networks and interactions that will put money in your pocket.

5. Invest In Digital Assets

This is another amazing way to make money during a financial meltdown. There are several other authors who may proffer relocating abroad, getting another nationality or securing offshore accounts as a way of escaping the bad situation that may have befallen the economy of your country. One thing you should note is that these advices are in fact, very valid, but you should also note that not everybody has the capability of following them.

Furthermore, acquiring these securities may come off as really expensive or with a lot of difficulties compared to other options that may exist. One of these options are digital assets. These digital assets are existent in binary arrangements and they can be used in trading and transactional communications. People often misinterpret other data as digital assets. Any data that does not come with a right to use for trade and transactions is not considered as an asset. Although these digital assets are not limited to these, they exist as documents, audio and video files, digital appliances and cryptocurrency.

Digital assets are financially valued as they represent merchandises being sold by businesses to consumers. The worth of these types of assets rise in accordance with their convention.

For people who cannot afford the luxury of relocating or sending money overseas for value preservation, digital assets are an option that can be used to earn profitably during a recession. For instance, you can check through the types of cryptocurrencies that exist and then, compare the more bullish ones. You can also conveniently trade them from any part of the world without having to receive permission from the government or any form of law enforcement. Trading digital assets are totally legal.

The Bottom Line

Commercial crises are absolutely inevitable as they occur occasionally. It may interest you to know that the 20th century recorded about twenty perceptible economic downturns. They may have been caused by various global calamities such as, terrorist attacks, international disputes or even socioeconomic issues. These events are the principal causes of distress and terror experienced by many people. Under such pressure, people tend to take irrational decisions in an attempt to put themselves in a safe spot. Consequentially, there are people who can keep their head straight with attitudes of calmness and discipline thereby analyzing the situation in order to understand the best and most rational steps to take. In situations like these, you have to make sure that you are part of these cool-headed category as it is the best way to amass success and wealth during the trying times. Rather than panic like the madding crowd, exercise discipline and patience, then analyze the situation so that you can take advantage of the opportunities that stand before you. Another vital aspect is your timing as you cannot afford to procure premature or delayed investments. The inaccuracy of this factor may decrease your impending advantages.

CHAPTER FOUR

TOP BILLIONAIRES WHO HAVE MADE MONEY DURING RECESSION

An economic recession is that business cycle period when the economy of a nation or nations experiences negative growth, often caused by industrial offsets such as oil price spike, financial panics, etc. The National Bureau of Economic Research in the United States defines a recession as *"a period of falling economic activity spread across the economy, lasting more than a few months."* I presume by now that, you already have an idea of the magnitude of its damaging effect. It affects firms and businesses financially, which might lead them to bankruptcy. Sales diminish because of the drop-in consumer demand and purchase. Subsequently, manufacturers and companies stop hiring new workers and even go as far as laying off a fraction of their old employees, which causes a sharp rise in the rate of unemployment. The effect of recession can be long-lasting even if it just lasted for a short period.

As stated by the IMF (International Monetary Funds), since the Second World War, four occasions of global recession have hit the world at large starting from 1975, 1982, 1991 and 2009. The last downturn which occurred between the year 2007 and 2009 had the most noticeable and broadest impact of them all; often called the Great Recession. It had four consecutive quarters of negative GDP growth. Its impact was massive such that the world economy is reportedly still slowly recovering from its effect and distress since 2010. Economic downturns such as GDP contractions, unemployment, businesses declaring bankruptcy, and the decrease in demand for homes followed suit during the recession although the impact varied from nations to nations. While some countries experienced swift and quite good recovery, others, however, experienced much slower recovery.

There are some set of people who were able to make lemonade out of the lemons of the financial recession by successfully turning the global curse to a blessing. To them, it was as if the downturn in the past never happened. These people were still able to make much more money for themselves in spite of the bitter financial situation the global village was in. Chuka Umunna, a Labor MP and member of the Treasury select committee, said: _"Clearly we are not all in this together."_ While many struggled through the bitter experience of recession, it was reported that _"the UK's 1,000 richest people increased in financial net worth."_ as stated by the Sunday Times Rich List. The question lies, who are they and what did they do differently?

Listed below are some of the billionaires who showed and executed remarkable approaches and timing during the recession period.

Warren Buffett

Warren Buffett is an American businessman, investor, and philanthropist. He is reckoned amongst the world's most prosperous financiers. He reportedly purchased his first stock at the age of eleven. The reputable business mogul and Berkshire Hathaway CEO, Warren Buffett says, _"Even dramatic shifts in the market don't have to be cause for concern."_ Buffett believes and always emphasizes holding onto investments long-term if you want to make remarkable success. In 2008, when the financial recession caused an equity fall, Warren released an article in The New York Times, expressing his intentions and business actions of buying American stock. He said this, _"Be fearful when others are greedy, and be greedy when others are fearful."_ He kept a level head even in the event of a massive credit crisis.

He made a difference with the decisions he took during the economic crises period as opposed to other investors who were lurching in utter fear. This further reiterated the philanthropist's business acumen. The investments he made include, the purchase of five billion dollars in preferred shares with Goldman Sachs which gave him ten percent returns and it also got him warrants to buy additional Goldman shares. He also acquired stock worth about $3 billion which had a tradeable 10% turnover at 10% premium with General Electric. He then, procured billions in redeemable shares at Swiss Re and Dow Chemical. All these companies were feeling the heat of the financial inferno, and so, they needed funds to survive the boisterous commercial crisis. As a result of his investment, while others cowered in during this period, he made billions of dollars in return and even provided help for other American firms while the recession lasted.

This exemplifies that Warren Buffett is a patient and methodical investor who smartly analyzed the impending situation in order to figure out the best things to invest in and then, grabbed the bull by the horn. He took a reasonable risk and now enjoys the yields. You can also emulate this act.

Sergey Brin

Sergey Brin was born in Moscow, Russia, and later moved to the United States. He is a co-founder of the renowned company Google Inc., alongside his friend Larry Page. Google Incorporation, which is an American public corporation, earns its revenue from advertisements related to internet search. The organization was one of the few establishments that did not experience a downturn during the recession. Its growth never took a halt, but they continued to grow through investments in a series of new product developments, acquisitions, partnerships, and so on. The profitable investments made by Google shows how beneficial it is to invest in digital assets as they are usually unaffected by the market crash.

Sergey Brin earned decent proceeds during the recession due to the increase in revenue generation recorded by the firm. This quickly exhibits that your pocket can be more potent when your business booms.

John Paulson

John Alfred Paulson is also an American investor, fund manager and philanthropist. He founded his investment management company Paulson and Co. in 1994, which he also leads. John Paulson made his fortune and prominence ironically during the financial crises bubble in 2007 when he placed a bet against the U.S. housing market. His bet against the housing market yielded an estimated $2.5 billion for his firm during the crisis. This yield magically transformed him from an average money manager into an investment legend. In 2009, he predicted an imminent financial recovery which earned him a multi-billion-dollar statuses in Goldman Sachs and Bank of America. In the year 2010, Paulson reportedly earned 4.9 billion dollars.

From these investments, you would realize that making money from financial crisis requires that you take risks. These risks have to be calculated so as to not usher in losses.

Jamie Dimon

Jamie Dimon is the CEO of the renowned JPMorgan Chase, the largest bank in the United States in terms of market capitalization. Jamie Dimon is considered one of the most financially successful bank executives who became a billionaire. His tremendous achievement can be credited to his stake in the JP Morgan.

During the great recession, Jamie made good use of the crisis by taking over banks that were under the wire due to the concurrent financial. Recently, he explained that action as a deliberate step taken to help the country and strengthen the company rather than to selfishly make a profit. Regardless of whatever motive he had, the level gave him a considerable gain in returns for JP Morgan. During the heat of the financial crisis, Dimon helped to foster the acquisition of the investment bank Bear Stearns, a company with $300 billion worth of assets, and the retail banking assets of Washington Mutual popularly called WaMu for JPMorgan. Those purchases later led to the profound reason why JPMorgan is among the leaders in market capitalization. Since the moment these massive economic decisions were taken, with cognizance to the crisis in 2008, JP Morgan had tripled its possession of shares which inversely made shareholders and its CEO quite wealthier than they were.

Steven Schonfeld

Steven Schonfeld is a billionaire, financial strategic advisor and trader. He is also the founder of his firm, Schonfeld Strategic Advisors, a multi-manager proprietary trading firm that trades across fundamental equity and tactical trading strategies. He was one of the benefactors of the global financial crises. His firm Schonfeld Group Holdings LLC supposedly acquired approximately $1 billion during the meltdown period. In one of his interviews after the recession, he said, *"You have to learn how to protect your wins, how to trade out of a loss and when to trade more and when to trade less."*

As a trading strategy, he believes that every investor should patiently invest in a five to seven-year time horizon, but eventually, if a financier decides to be a trader, then, the holding time can be truncated by approximately 50 percent. Evidentially, the financial crisis seemed to have worked out in Steven Schonfeld's advantage as palpable in the profits he amassed during the period.

Andrew Beal

Andrew Beal made the list of gainers during the great economic tumult. Andrew is an American banker, businessman and investor. He made his wealth through investments in real estate and banking having estimated a net-worth of 9.3 billion dollars as at February 2019. He tripled his net worth to 4.5 billion dollars during the meltdown by purchasing mortgage securities and failed loans.

Carl Icahn

Carl Icahn is an American based businessman. He founded the Icahn Enterprise, a holding company with various portfolios. According to Forbes magazine, Icahn had a net worth of 17 billion dollars in 2019 making him the 26th wealthiest man on the Forbes 400 list. Just as other successful investors did during the meltdown, Icahn did not cower in by selling, he invested. Here is a list of his investments between 2006 and 2010.

- August 2006: He invested in stocks in the video game publisher "Take-Two interactive" and later increased his holdings to 11.3% in 2009, thus making him the company's largest shareholder.

- January 2007: He bought a 9.2% stake at Telik, a biotech company.

- February 2007: He offered Lear Corporation's board of directors a $2.3 billion as a buy-off of the company.

- Also, in 2007, he sold three of his properties for approximately 1.3 billion dollars which was many times the money he invested in purchasing the assets.

During the peak of the financial crises, Icahn made a lot of massive investments and calculated sales which profited Him enormously. This man I rather call the business mogul of hard times. Come another recessive, it is highly likely Icahn record another massive gain.

In case making money during recession had sounded like a myth to you, these people listed above leveraged the crisis into a money-making period. Are you not amused that certain people were gainers during a time when the global village, was suffering from an economic meltdown such that everything seemed to be collapsing? These people and many others were able to add to their fortune as some millionaires became billionaires for the first time. After realizing the extent at which these people had profited from the sad austerity period, I reckon that you lose your fears and surge forth on investments.

According to a report gathered by many independent experts such as the Institute for Fiscal Studies, it was discovered that the impact an economic recession is falling heavier on lower-income families and middle Britain.

In all the above people mentioned to have profited from financial downturn, you would notice that they all have differences in the types of commerce they venture into. Nonetheless, they all share some similarities which include, patience, calmness, discipline and passion. These moguls successfully used these tools to take high and calculated risks without cowering and that resulted into incredible gains for them.

Conclusively, it was highly evident that the great recession of 2008 influenced market crashes, which made the world collectively lose wealth worth trillions of dollars. However, knowledgeable investors perceived the crash in the stock market as a golden opportunity to purchase the shares that many companies were letting go at cheap sale rates. As markets have recovered from the Great Recession, these investors have realized tremendous gains from their assertive maneuvers.

Assertively, you should not cower in the face of financial crisis, instead, explore the opportunities that are available before you.

CONCLUSION

MAINTAINING YOUR SUCCESS

The idea of being a millionaire discussed in this book means more than just having a certain amount carrying six zeros sitting comfortably in your bank account. It speaks more about being a wealthy and successful person at large. It is one thing to possess money that can be exhausted in a matter of time, and it is another thing to own securities that will ensure you a lifetime of wealth. To some people, the moment they have a prominent figure in the bank, their dreams have been made while there are others who believe that life has just started. This explains that there are differences in the ways people define success. How do you define success? What level will you attain in life before you consider yourself successful?

Have you answered these above questions in your head, or you have difficulties providing answers to them? This is because the first step to take towards being successful and prosperous is to, first of all, define your type of success. This will be the gauge with which you will measure your progress in life.

There are many entrepreneurs who started businesses and have been unable to sustain its running for up to ten years. In this same scene, there are a lot of other companies that have been running for about forty years and are still active and stable. Of course, there is a difference in their descriptions of success. The difference between short-lived businesses and long-surviving ones is the power of the dream. People have aspirations about how and what they want their establishment to be, but not all these people have a full understanding of what it takes.

For a person who wishes to build a long-lasting venture, you would understand that it takes dedication, resilience, good character, discipline, zeal and hard work coupled with the knowledge that the desired feat cannot be achieved overnight.

Many entrepreneurs are often misguided by the first boom that occurs in the early years of business such that their focus is set on the present and plans for the future are not adequately made. In some other cases, the inability to weather the storm of financial obstacles is why many establishments fail quicker than expected. It is imperative to understand that sustaining a business to a level of immense wealth and success is challenging but achievable. Does the saying _"nothing good comes easy"_ make sense to you now?

One of the significant challenges encountered by entrepreneurs is the inability to withstand financial crises. These situations often set panic in the atmosphere such that people start to live in fear like it is the end of the world. The recession has the ability to unnerve many trades to an irredeemable weakness.

These challenges are part of the causes of collapsed business organizations.

As stated in the chapters of this book, surviving financial meltdowns start with you. You have to be calm and smart so as not to make the decisions that will leave your dreams in jeopardy. According to Warren Buffett, _"you only have to do a very few things right in your life so long as you don't do too many things wrong."_ Ensuring that you make the most out of negative financial situations is one of the right things to do to keep your dream of being a millionaire alive.

It is better to smartly overcome the barriers that exist between you and your success rather than wallow in the fear that you may never make it through as it may affect your chances. Doing things right involve knowing and valuing yourself and other people, protecting your reputation and executing a solid plan that will expedite the prolonged existence of your accomplishment.

In addition, you also have to create a balance in your life. You should plan and work hard towards achieving your dream, but this should not consume you. There is the need to infuse some flexibility in order to create a space for the brewing of ideas into reality. Lack of balance may attract redundancy, which is unacceptably detrimental to your aspiration. Therefore, you should create a poise that will help maintain your success.

There is a common mistake that a lot of entrepreneurs have made which has complicated their chances of attaining their desired success level. This mistake is the lack of path. A lot of people lose themselves under the disguise of followership. When venturing into business, it is smart to have a coach or mentor that will guide you to the top, but in this bid, do not lose your path. Mentees have a habit of following the exact footsteps of their mentor, and this often ends up where they do not want. Blindly following another person's path will expose you to the errors they committed, then, you will use the same solution they employed to escape the mistake and then, you take a turn and halt at the same endpoint they did.

You need to create a path for yourself so that you can explore your chances of attaining greater heights than your mentor. A coach should only guide you through your way and not lead you through theirs. Creating your path will give you a more excellent knowledge of how to maintain your success. It will help define your endeavors such that you fully understand how to manage the different situations that may arise.

Lastly, being a millionaire requires that you learn from your mistakes. Errors are inevitable as they occur from time to time, but you can reduce the reoccurrences to a minute level by ensuring that you fill the gaps that caused the previous ones.

Your ability to remain unaffected by the thorns of financial crises will aid your chances of being a millionaire.

www.ingramcontent.com/pod-product-compliance
Lightning Source LLC
Chambersburg PA
CBHW030728180526
45157CB00008BA/3090